In 1996 Firkin Crane initiated its ambitious Righting Dance programme. The opportunity and the challenge - both equally daunting and enormously rewarding - presented to Irish choreographers was to commit themselves to a process of research where their aesthetic vision and choreographic craft would be laid bare, examined, pushed and moved in new directions, towards new possibilities, leaving behind the certainties and safety of their accustomed practices.

introduction

Firkin Crane's ambition in the Righting Dance programme has been the re-invigoration of dance in Ireland. As a centre dedicated to the development of dance, Firkin Crane seeks to engineer circumstances that test and try current practice, helping to innovate stronger work and proposals for fresh approaches in making dance. Righting Dance was set up as a programme of rigorous choreographic investigation within the context of this broader vision. This book bears testimony to the success of its explorative spirit.

The articulation through the pages of this book of the research undertaken amounts to much more than a documentary record of the interchanges between dancers and dance makers. Writing Dancing - Righting Dance: Articulations on a Choreographic Process is in itself an integral, vital part of the research. Through the juxtaposition and interconnection of written text and visual imagery, it offers fresh insights into the subtleties and dynamics of choreography. It attempts to concretise the ephemerality of the process and, at the same time, interact evocatively with the process itself; a meeting across art forms.

There is much still to be understood about the art of choreography. It is a word that has gained increasing currency, entering common parlance in a range of different situations. Yet the complexities of this crucial process in dance remain largely hidden, often ignored. This book sets out to illuminate and enlighten. I am indebted to all who gave generously and with an open curiosity throughout the project.

Mary Brady
Artistic Director
(Spring 2000)

At the still point of the turning world. Neither flesh nor fleshless; Neither from nor towards; at the still point, there the dance is, But neither arrest nor movement. And do not call it fixity, Where past and future are gathered. Neither movement from nor towards, Neither ascent nor decline. Except for the point, the still point, There would be no dance, and there is only the dance...*

This is a story about choreographic process. About making dances. Dancing and writing share a common space. To choreograph is to write a dance into space. To write is to choreograph oneself on the page. Moving and writing as a way into (and out of) performance. The space of dance is a space of embodiment and erasure simultaneously. Words uttered and written, actions rendered and gestures released into the space/onto the page by choreographer, dancer and writer, urge each other forward into a personal and public archive for remembering, re-visiting, preserving. What is preserved is, of course, a fiction.

    *Eliot, T.S. Four Quartets, "Burnt Norton" Part II, New York: Harcourt, Brace and Company, 1943 (first published 1935)

All knowledge, experience, observation is mediated. There is no purely objective means of observation.
We are dealing here with the world between ourselves and others.*

Writing, a pen-pushing dance, a physical act, is constantly on the move through the space of seeing (sighting), imagining, seeking, rupturing,

and materially evoking. In the words of Julia Kristeva, writing down (performance) is an ordeal ... like love. An ordeal, like choreography.

The choreographic process happens as much by accident as by design. The unexpected, the surprise, the question - reveal something essential in a moment of intuitive knowing.

Over time, and with practice, a rigorous intuition leads the choreographer towards a seeing clearly and a feeling clearly in the moment-to-moment of making.

*Mcauley, Gay. "Towards an Ethnography of rehearsal". *New Theatre Quarterly* Vol. XIV-Number 53, February 1998

One step/gesture/impulse follows another and becomes a phrase. The phrase, worked, worn, discovered by the dancers, becomes more and more articulated. The articulation reveals an image, a shape within a rhythm, a vision within a shape that you can actually remember and play over in your mind, play over in the space. A dance is coming into existence, but only for a momentary life. The life of an ephemera. Perhaps in its repeating there is a change of heart in the collective dancer body. The image vanishes, the articulations collapse or disintegrate. Or perhaps the choreographer's fascination with the "text"(ure) is suspended in mid-flow as a new becoming is proposed.

Dancers, choreographers and writers spend a lot of time looking, witnessing, tracing with their eyes, mapping with their muscles. They are constantly absorbing, processing, taking in and trying out. They are constantly rehearsing, harrowing, turning over and over the soil for the planting of new ideas, for the making of new space in their bodies and in the force-field of their poly-logic energies.

January 18, 1999

Dear Tedd,

Thanks for your message. Really looking forward to the weekend....As a starting point for me this Righting Dance programme has to do with three "D's":

Dancemaking Dramaturgy Documentation

As artistic facilitator/mentor/monitor it strikes me that you are the question - asker, the one who is observing and also instigating challenges within the processes of the choreographers. The description of your role seems to me aligned with that of the dramaturg. The lovely little piece by Marianne van Kerkhoven called "Looking Without Pencil in the Hand" that I sent to Mary Brady and which you have probably seen, is apt here, I think. I want to ask you about those ways of seeing and thinking about choreography that you bring with you into the studio from your own work when you are working with Mary and Paul. The how and what of that space you inhabit, in between what you ask about your own work and what you see (in a new way) when looking at Paul and Mary working.

Any thoughts on this to start with would be fascinating as well as practical regarding how you see your brief in this project!

Best Wishes,

Diana

silent

journey

searching

subjectivity

synthesis

Uncertainty itself is the subject and focus of choreographers' work*

She sits out and watches the dancers for a while. Their arms are signalling cryptic codes to one

another across the space. She closes her eyes for a moment. Who is writing this dance?

How do all these arms know their particular story? How do they know what comes next?

Can they continue shaping the space without me? What journey are we on? "How can I lead

if I am the most lost person in the world?" (she will ask later, but not now). There is an ethos of

silence here broken only by the sound of my pencil and hers skittering across flat white surfaces,

and of the breath and feet of the dancers, sometimes laboured, sometimes mercurial.

Tedd encourages everyone to talk less. To be silent. To show rather than to discuss.

"Being mindful about words, using them only to help rather than to confuse."

 *Gilpin, Heidi. "Shaping Critical Spaces: Issues in the Dramaturgy of Movement Performance" in *Dramaturgy in American Theatre: A source book* eds. Susan Jonas, Geoff Proehl, Michael Lupu. Harcourt Brace College Publishers,1997

Hi Tedd!

Hello Diana,

Hope this finds you thriving. I am working on the documentation for the Righting Dance Project (slow because of so much other work and also new thoughts on what/how it is to serve has kept things rather fluid).

Yes, thriving perhaps, just finishing my season, two weeks to go, one here in Montreal premiering new work for some students (sounds like a small task but most of the dance milieu here go to see this end of year performance, so there is some pressure to make it interesting) and then off to première a new work for a solo artist in Regina. Then I can start on my new solo in June.

While you were in residence at Firkin Crane did you meet with the dancers on a daily basis (without the choreographers)?

This is true. With the experiences that I have had with dancers, I thought this might be a good method of keeping them informed and they, in turn, keeping me informed of how they were and any suggestions they might have for more efficiency in the working process.

Can you please talk to me about those discussions?

The methods that I employ are usually related to what is happening at the time, as each situation is quite different. I sometimes adapt methods that have "worked" before. The "functional talking" assignment is adapted from zen training. I could see that with Mary and Paul, and the dancers, from interaction with them, that these people talked a lot. Words can be confusing as they are not "the dance"; in fact, I think that differing parts of the brain functions are used for movement and words. Since we were investigating movement, I felt that it might be interesting to allow the choreographers a chance to vent their creative energy through actual movement rather than allowing ideas to be expressed in words, thus draining some of the creative energy away from the movement expression. As this was difficult for Mary and Paul, I had to impose silence on them to block their natural and unrecognised venting of nervous energy through talking. We only did this a couple of times in order for them to experience the usefulness of the exercise, so that they could then employ it when needed. All agreed that it was a useful exercise....

Best Wishes,

Tedd!

"Talking is talking **Dancing is dancing...**

alking is not dancing

Dancing is not talking...

Dancing is talking.

Talking is dancing"*

*Douglas Dunn, "Talking Dancing" in Banes, Sally. *Terpsichore in Sneakers*. Boston: Houghton Mifflin Company, 1977.

THE WALLS OF THE STUDIO AT FIRKIN CRANE ARE OF BLUE YELLOW AQUA WITH RED HEAT LAMPS BRIGHT
BANKS OF LIGHTS ON STAGE FACING THE STUDIO FLOOR TO SIMULATE DAYLIGHT FOR VIDEO TAPING AND
PHOTOGRAPHIC WORK BY DEREK SPIERS MARY AND TEDD ARE IN THE SPACE WORKING WITH THE FIVE
DANCERS TEDD WEARING HIS FLOWING BLACK MONK'S ROBE MARY IS RUNNING THROUGH BITS OF
MATERIAL WITH THE DANCERS SHE STANDS WITH HER WEIGHT SOLIDLY ON BOTH FEET IN DEMI-PLIÉ
PARALLEL ARMS CROSSED THE MEN PERFORM SHORT CHOPPED BREATHY PHRASES PERCUSSIVE
ATTACKS WHICH PEETER OUT AND BREAK APART THE WOMEN PERFORM CURVACEOUS
PHRASES WITH TENSIONS AND PULLS ACROSS THEIR BODIES WHILE THEIR
TRAVELLING MOTION LIKE FINGERPAINTING SMEARS THE SPACE AND MARKS THE
TIME AS THEY TRY OUT DIFFERENT ORDERS TEMPERAMENTS DYNAMICS IN THE
PHRASES MARY SAYS BE AS CALM AS YOU CAN POSSIBLY BE IN THAT...HUM A
LITTLE TUNE THE MOVEMENT GATHERS UP THE SPACE WITH ARMS VERY
SUSTAINED SUSPENSEFUL AS THEY LIFT AND THEN WHOO! BIG RELEASE OF
AUDIBLE BREATH ARMS SLASH WITH GREAT PHYSICAL FORCE AND
MOMENTUM RÍONACH DANCES SOLO IN THE SPACE AND FINDS HER WAY
INTO THE MOVEMENT TEDD HAS SUDDENLY VANISHED AND RE-APPEARS
BUSTLING INTO THE STUDIO WITH A FAX IN IRISH FOR RÍONACH A POP SONG
BLARES OUT FROM THE NEXT STUDIO FROM THE KIDDIE JAZZ CLASS THE
OTHER DANCERS CARRY ON PROGRESSING THROUGH AND THROUGHOUT THE SPACE WITH THEIR BREATHY
SLASHY REACHY ELONGATED PHRASES WITH BURSTS OF MOMENTUM-FILLED PROPULSIONS INTO A CURVE-
REACH-CURVE-REACH-SLASH-CURVE-PIVOT SEQUENCES AS IF VOICES FROM UNDER THE FLOORBOARDS
COMPEL THEM TO LISTEN THEY MOMENTARILY PAUSE THEIR BODIES IN A STATE OF LISTENING AND
ALERTNESS THEN THEY MOVE ON THEN BEGINS A SLOW PUSH AROUND OF A QUARTET INTO DUOS TRIOS
AND TO SOLOS JAKE AND RÍONACH PERFORM A DUET THAT IS FULL OF LOVELY LITTLE ETIQUETTES
RESISTANCES CHEEKY TOUCHES HE SHRUGS A SHOULDER SHE PUSHES IT DOWN HE MOVES HER
PONYTAIL CLEARS A SPACE FOR HIMSELF THEY PLAY LIKE PUPPIES MARY SHOUTS OUT HEY TEDD ANY

EAS ABOUT MUSIC DEREK KEEPS PHOTOGRAPHING EVERYONE INCLUDING ME WRITING AND CLODAGH SHOOTING E VIDEO CAMERA THE DANCERS REHEARSE THE SEQUENCES AND PHRASES LIKE A ROSARY 2 OF THESE THEN OF THOSE IT'S 5:25 PM. THE DANCERS HAVE BEEN WORKING ALL DAY AND BECAUSE MY PLANE WAS LATE EY ARE KINDLY WORKING ON INTO THE EVENING ANDY IS SAYING THAT HE MUST HAVE BEEN WORKING IN E OTHER STUDIO WITH PAUL WHILE A CERTAIN PHRASE WAS BEING TAUGHT BECAUSE HE FEELS IN THE RK UNFAMILIAR WITH IT HE FEELS AT SEA BUT IS GOOD HUMOURED ABOUT IT RELAXED AND PUSHES ROUGH IT WITH PANACHE MEANWHILE TEDD HAS CONJURED UP SOME MUSIC AND THEY BEGIN A RUN ROUGH OF THE MATERIAL SO FAR A HANDEL ARIA SUNG BY A COUNTER TENOR I LIKE THE TERM ASTRATI AND JESSE NORMAN SINGING SCHUBERT VERY BAUSCHIAN I THINK WONDERFUL DISTINCT RSONAS AND SHAPES EMERGE IN THE DANCING THE CRIPPLE THE ANGEL THE STREET URCHIN THE IMATE THE MOVEMENTS PROMOTE BUTTS AND ARMS WITH ATTITUDE AS THEY ALL EXHALE SHARPLY D PERFORM TIGHT LITTLE MOTIFS AROUND THEIR OWN BODY SPHERES THEN PERFORM WHOA! STOP! ESTURES WITH THEIR ARMS AS THEY STOP IN MID-AIR BEFORE COLLIDING THE ACTIONS MELT AND MOULD SLOWLY INTO AND AROUND EACH OTHER WITH LONG TAFFY PULLS I'M THINKING ABOUT HAYDN D HOW HIS WIT WOULD WORK SO WELL HERE SO! MARY EXCLAIMS LOOKING AT HER WATCH AT THE END THE RUN TEDD ALWAYS WORKS WITH BAROQUE MUSIC OR BACH IN PROCESS WHICH HE CALLS POWDER USIC AS A GOOD TEST IF IT DOESN'T WORK WITH THAT YOU KNOW YOU'VE GOT TO LOOK AT THE MATERIAL GAIN HE FEELS IT GIVES DEFINITION TO MOVEMENT HELPS TO SEE WHAT IT IS HE AGREES ABOUT HAYDN AND ANS TO BRING IN A HAYDN STRING QUARTET HE'S A PORTABLE SOUND ARCHIVE HE SAYS HE ONLY HAS TEN CDS ARY ASKS FOR LEONARD COHEN A DANCER IS HORRIFIED AND CRIES OUT NO! FATHER TEDD THEY CALL TO HIM R HELP LET'S GO...NOW HE SAYS AND THEY START DANCING AGAIN A PULSY PERCOLATING REICH OR GLASS ECE OF MUSIC STARTS TO FILL THE SPACE BUILDING FILLING DRIVING RÍONACH SHUDDERS THEN FRACTURES INTO TS OF SMALL BODY ISOLATIONS THEN TURNS THEN STRETCHES LUXURIOUSLY THE PHRASE PLAYFUL AND SELF-SORBED REMINDS ME WHY I LOVE WATCHING DANCE, RENEWS DANCE FOR ME THE HUMAN FORM CELEBRATING OVEMENT MOMENT TO MOMENT BEING IN TIME AND SPACE AND COMMUNICATING SOMETHING ABOUT THE FORT AND WILL AND ORGANISATION IT TAKES TO GO ON TO KEEP MOVING.

THIS PROJECT IS VERY HARD WORK, NOT FOR THE FAINT HEARTED. IT IS ABOUT BEING IN RETREAT BUT
ALSO BEING ON THE LINE: WORK, REFLECT, LEARN, DO, MAKE, RE-MAKE, DRAFT, RE-DRAFT. HOW TO FIND
THE ESSENTIAL SOMETHING THAT SIGNALS YOUR MOTIVATION TO MAKE? WHAT ENDURES AFTER EACH DRAFT?
WHAT DO YOU DESIRE? HOW DO YOU RECOGNISE NEW VOCABULARY, NEW MEANS WHEN YOU SEE IT?
SUCH A PRIVILEGE AND SUCH A RESPONSIBILITY - TO WORK HARD AND TO BE OBSERVED AND TO CONFRONT
YOUR OWN CRAFT IN THE MAKING AND IN THE CHANGING.

Righting Dance invites established Irish choreographers (established? what is established? what establishment?)
into a laboratory setting where they can re-assess where they are, what they want to do next, and re-consider their
working process in dialogue with a choreographic 'mentor'. The dialogue can be a series of 'interventions' or
'provocations' about their work that destabilises their habitual practices, or a menu of tasks, assigned and shared,
or a kind of intensive feedback structure or critical playing/interrogating of the material in progress.

Established at the Firkin Crane Dance Development Agency under the direction of Mary Brady, and having completed two such projects to date, Righting Dance is the only such venture in Ireland. The project is about valuing the untapped potential in choreographers/makers, about recognising the constant funding pressures that choreographers labour under and about the notion of the choreographer as **producer** of work rather than as a **researcher** of an art form. In the production culture of professional choreographers there is a continuing denial of space for reflection and analysis. A field work period needs a reflection period. Professional choreographers have evolved the skills they need to produce work within only several weeks of making and rehearsing time. Economics make this so. But what skills have choreographers *suppressed* in doing so?

As a way of fostering, nurturing, promoting, and developing choreographic stature in this country, the Righting Dance programme needs to be undertaken again and again and again. Each project is, in essence, a 'draft' of conditions, aims and objectives and these projects, over time, will create a map of developments, preoccupations and opportunities for choreographic style and identity.

This document textualises the working processes between choreographers Paul Johnson (MaNDaNCE, Dublin) and Mary Nunan (Daghdha Dance Company, University of Limerick) in dialogue with their mentor, the venerable Tedd Senmon-Robinson (Artistic Director, 10 Gates Dancing Inc., Ottawa, Canada) and with dancers Jake McLellan, Andy Papas, Richard O'Brien, Ríonach Ní Neill and Lisa Mc Loughlin. The project started in January, 1999, and ran for three weeks.*

*The Righting Dance Project was launched in 1997, documented, recorded and evaluated as 'Time Out 1' with choreographer, Adrienne Brown and mentor, Kim Brandstrup. For information on this project and an introduction to the Righting Dance Programme see the report: Righting Dance: Time Out by Finola Cronin, December, 1997, commissioned by Firkin Crane with financial support from the Calouste Gulbenkian Foundation. Copies can be obtained from the Firkin Crane - Dance Development Agency, Shandon, Cork.

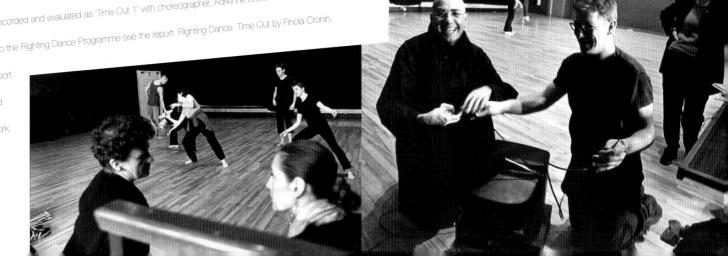

Righting Dance is a mapping of choreographic journeys. It is an imagined and real set of dialogues between choreographers, dancers, and mentors. Between movers, makers and writers. It looks at documentation as a method of prising open, framing, following new leads about connections between dance and its process, about authorship of choreographing/dancing/writing. It places something into an arena for looking.

It is reportage.
It is a chronicling.

It is an inventory. It is a testament.
It is a witnessing. It is a fiction.

It is a counter-text to the choreographic process.

Part of performance...

Part of performance research must surely be the attempt to document process. The opening up of systems of writing, systems of rehearsing, and relationships between practice and theory all point towards a livelier, more expansive notion of research in and of performance. But how do we proceed to document working processes? Many layers are called upon: the observation of the work itself - a live, durational witnessing; the video camera; the audio recording; the transcribing of recordings; diaries/logs/journals of makers; dialogues; interviews. The activity of writing down all observations in order to reflect on constructions, questions, patterns. The 'logic' that emerges from the fluidities of material shaped from intuition, prescription, discovery. The translation through many selves : alert, active, pressured, tightened, accelerated, fatigued, blinded. Each of these layers and each of these selves privileges different points of perspective of the subject - the process itself.

And despite the tools of documentation, especially the recording tools of video and camera, (conversations between eye and hand of the camera operators, Clodagh Kelly - video, and Derek Spiers - photography) the rehearsal process is a highly verbal, highly oral activity.

Much of the 'narrative' takes place in private as much as in public space. The invisible spaces as well as the visible. It takes place in coffee breaks, in whispers close together between choreographer and mentor, in the 'second thought' moments, alone with the day's after-images, in eruptions of laughter at the end of a "run" of material, and in the countless nooks and crannies in the construction that is choreography. Recording. Preserving. Translating. Interpreting.

It is all a fragile and delicate business, constantly beckoning questions of usefulness and truthfulness of documentation. Choreographer, dancer, mentor, writer all engage in a constant back and forth movement between rehearsal, performance, the writing down and the talking through. At every moment we are enacting a ritual of bringing something into existence that was not there before.

A choreographer's description of process:

"This work has been tampered with, sweaty hands of many people, worked over and over, questioned, worn down, until it's become something else. What I look at now in my mind seems a strange and tangled thing, and as I write, it changes still more under my gaze, day by day. Each thought I have entwines itself within the original flesh, and each day, on coming back to it, I'm less and less sure which is mine and which is not." (Eleanor Brickhill)

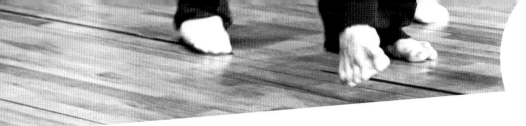

In my position of 'intimate distance' from where I view the chaos of creation, my eyes and pencil impose an order on my seeing. Apollo in the temple of Dionysus (as Joe Orton said). I write continuously, am seen to be writing continuously. Mary and Paul and Tedd and the dancers become familiar with the 'backround energy' of my note-taking. I am constantly rehearsing the act of "perceptive doing".*

The writing is an extension of the 'performance', born out of the desire to "capture the flow of circling meaning"** that is the very weave of choreography.

* De Marinis, Marco "Dramaturgy of the Spectator" *The Drama Review* Vol.31, No. 2 1987

** Adolphe, Jean-Marc. 'Dramaturgy of Movement' *Ballet International/Tanz Akeull* Vol. 6, 1998

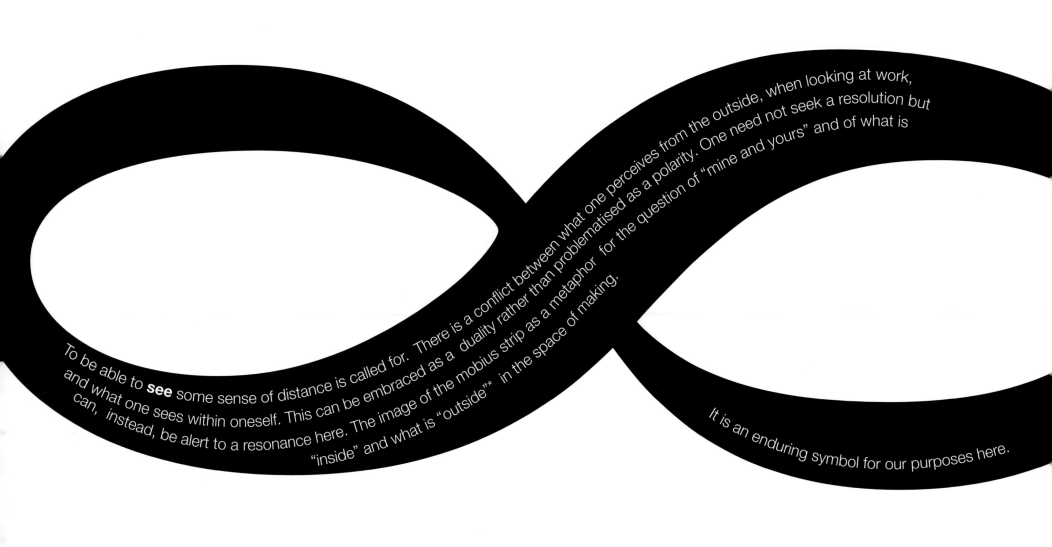

To be able to **see** some sense of distance is called for. There is a conflict between what one perceives from the outside, when looking at work, and what one sees within oneself. This can be embraced as a duality rather than problematised as a polarity. One need not seek a resolution but can, instead, be alert to a resonance here. The image of the mobius strip as a metaphor for the question of "mine and yours" and of what is "inside" and what is "outside"* in the space of making.

It is an enduring symbol for our purposes here.

* Cole, Susan Letzler, *Directors in Rehearsal*. London: Routledge, 1992

of the work and also the movement material.

Hello Tedd,

The prospect of having the space and time to work, under the guidance of a mentor, for 3 weeks is very exciting. The fact that there is no pressure to produce a finished work at the end of the 3 weeks is wonderful. It affords me the option of going into the process without my habitual approach to creating choreography, an approach which has been formed as a result of working under my "normal" choreographic conditions, i.e. a predetermined number of weeks to create and produce a finished piece. I know that I have become quite efficient at doing that well, but I feel that there must be numbers of creative options that are never explored, simply because there isn't the time. So January provides that opportunity.

One issue on which I would like to focus as part of the Project is that of artistic impulse. How to listen to it, sense it and how to translate it into some kind of form, without imposing form on it. I know that this is a life long process but I hope to make some advances in this process in January. To date the works I have created have all been an attempt to translate personal experiences, perceptions or "philosophies" into choreography. Sometimes the impulses have been primarily visceral / emotional, other times more intellectual / reflective. As a result the choreography can take quite different forms - some works have been very direct and forceful with a strong "physical theatre" dimension, others (the more recent works) have tended to be more lyrical and with pure movement orientation. I believe Peter Boneham was wondering was I a bit schizophrenic when he saw the videos of the works! And worse than that, I must admit I have even wondered that myself.

But no, because despite their different manifestations I do think there is a thread that runs through them. This thread is the sense/essence/heart of the work and also the movement of material. Looking back at the material I realise that it has really evolved to become much more textured with a wider dynamic range, with a result that in the last work I choreographed - "Chimera" - I focused more than ever before on listening to what the movement material needed in terms of development rather than being led by the dramatic and emotional themes which were actually the initial impulse for the work.

So moving on to the next work I would like to research this further - using the materials of movement (Body, Space, Rhythm, Time, Dynamics, Relationship, Stillness - and so on) as the starting point for the choreography.

The aim would be to create work with its own inherent logic and intelligence driven by a kinetic sensibility and not dependent on an emotional or intellectual theme as its starting point. So then the big question for me is where do I start ...... perhaps with your suggestion of the development of vocabulary for the left thumb?!

But additionally, as well as the challenge of starting with movement as the impulse, I also want to bear in mind that ultimately I would like this to work not only for me but that, when choreographed into a final piece, it will have the ability to communicate straight to the core of the audiences and cut right through all overly active dramatic, emotional and intellectual expectations to a profound and refreshingly new space deep within them! So now...

Sincerely,
Mary

Dear Peter,

...... I understand that you have seen some bio/resume.....information that will not be found but nevertheless is very important - I'm 33 years of age, gay and happily involved in a secure and loving relationship. I smoke, drink and enjoy an active social life outside of dance, would describe myself as confident, intelligent and inquisitive. Passionately interested in all of the arts, I read, cook and keep a mean house!! Sounds like a personal ad..... I like myself, my body and do not have a problem with most things, i.e. being gay, dysfunctional family or a burning desire to rule the world.

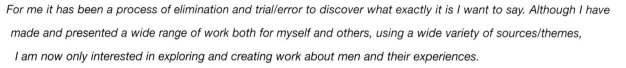

Fragment of a letter from Paul Johnson to Peter Boneham, Artistic Director at Le Groupe de la Place Royale, Ottawa, Canada, before joining the Righting Dance Programme.

After twelve years working as a dancer, teacher and choreographer I feel I am only now fully realising what it is exactly I want to achieve for myself in dance. My career has come full circle in most ways and I now find myself just wanting to concentrate exclusively on my own work as a choreographer/performer.

For me it has been a process of elimination and trial/error to discover what exactly it is I want to say. Although I have made and presented a wide range of work both for myself and others, using a wide variety of sources/themes, I am now only interested in exploring and creating work about men and their experiences.

MaNDaNCE as an ethos/initiative came out of a desire to create work that challenged the male stereotype. I want as a male to explore many aspects of what it is to be a man today - not exclusively from one or other angle - I want to formulate a way of choreographically presenting original devised works that inform and contribute intelligently to dance practice in Ireland.

I get tired of some of the labels and myths I see presented on stage and want simply to be able to present alternatives.

At this moment in my work I feel/realise I would greatly benefit from the opportunity to further experiment in a research/development period under the guidance/in collaboration with someone/third eye/mentor. A lot of my work, from 1990 onwards, was developed in isolation through rigorous rehearsals and work-in-progress presentations. I learned very much as I went along - valuable and at the time necessary because there was no one around I could confidently work with. The more I worked the better I became at identifying and honing my ideas and then the better I became at expressing them and now I can work clearly with other dancers on realising my choreography. But I know I need to do more and not exactly sure how best to do this....

With regards and best wishes,

Yours sincerely,

Paul Johnson

Paul:

I want to engage in the choreographic dialogue of working with Mary, not in the same studio but working simultaneously in different studios, sharing the dancers.

Mary:

I want to look at my choreographic process, experiment, see what themes present themselves.

Paul:

I want feedback from Tedd, then have dialogue with Mary. How can I creatively address blocks when they occur in my process? I want to scrutinise my own way of making work. Most of the pieces I make are in isolation - the dialogue has essentially stopped, in that my company members are tuned in but nowhere, in a kind of auto-pilot mode. Working with dancers unknown to me, opening up new ways of communicating, freeing myself up from issue-based, political work. The ethos of my work can remain but I want to change tactics.

Mary:

From punk (my need to punch, break, smash something apart)...
to carpenter where I feel it, turn it (movement) like wood.

Tedd:

Devising new tasks for these choreographers has been different
from the Laboratory in Canada. Here there are more tasks,
smaller bits than would usually happen. Here we are really looking
closely at ways of doing things and opening up/challenging habits
of making.

some task examples:

Make a movement phrase on the spot, minus the travelling. Identify what is the essence of the phrase.

Work with tableau in non-unison and address the 'dynamic flatness'. Start material with an emotion

- e.g. anger, and find the energy of anger. Make a movement phrase and then ask. Have you ever done

anything like this before? Create a movement phrase and explore how to put texture into it. Try breathing

through it differently. Try working through it backwards. Break from the phrase then maintain the phrase.

Introduce a gesture into the phrase.

There was some resistance to these tasks. It is very difficult to take them on, absorb them immediately. How do you take ownership of a task you don't feel is very interesting'?

The dancers are voicing choice about the work they do.

What is the interaction between the dancers?

What are their expectations, motivations?

How do they own and perform the material?

Can they go on a journey to the unknown with the choreographer?

Do they have their own agendas?

Over the past three weeks I feel that I have become increasingly sympathetic towards Mary and Paul. Both choreographers have, at times, been vulnerable and fragile, as they have attempted to make changes to their choreographic style and process. This has, for me, created an unusual power structure in the studio between the dancers and the choreographers.

The dancers, for instance, can no longer look to the choreographers for clear instructions as the choreographers are entering into new choreographic territory which they are not always sure how to verbalise. The dancers are also seeing the choreographers in a far more 'human' and personal way as the choreographers struggle with the challenges that Tedd places upon them. The dancers, therefore, see the choreographers swing from being happy to sad, confident to frustrated etc.; there is no sense of the 'distanced' relationship which often occurs between dancers and choreographers. The dancers are then often seeing the choreographers in a weakened state, without their usual confidence, vision and drive.

I decided, because of the fragility of both choreographers, to be as sensitive as possible to the needs of both choreographers. I felt that, in the studio, I should be simply a body which is adaptable... to the choreography without any questioning.

be able to experiment

be flexible in their thinking

be able to kinesthetically switch over

from one choreographer to another

witness the mentor in dialogue with

the choreographer

use improvisation skills within the

tasks Tedd proposes

observe each other in the work

be alert bodies

be adventurous human beings

be very patient

The Laboriousness of Documentation

"The sheer bulk of material that accumulates in one short project; the hours and hours of video tapes, the stacks of notes, the cassettes that eventually must be transcribed, the photographs, the correspondence, the hastily noted conversations over a drink, the glimpses of logbooks, diaries, journals of all the participants, the remembering. This small museum in and of memory is not easily accessed nor sifted. It's imprinted, like the cartographer in the Borges story whose map was so .... detailed that it eventually became co-extensive with the territory it mapped."* In what way is this documentation a tool for this project? A counter text of the process? Proposals for new choreographic vocabulary? Poetic reportage? Scoring for improvisational research? This is vulnerable research. The writer attempts to illuminate events about choreographic process by writing *amidst* choreographic process.

* Mcauley, Gay."Towards an Ethnography of Rehearsal". *New Theatre Quarterly*, Vol. XIV No. 53, February1998

The project is driven from the perspective of the choreographers. On how they view their working practice in Ireland. This is a 'time out' - a space for personal rather than market pressures - to explore, experiment, reflect on, interrogate, bust open - the ways of making they habitually engage in - to take a departure point, to find a moment that feels "new".

Exposure of the Choreographer

Questions for Paul @ 11 a.m. January 28th

What was a discovery you made
in your process here?

"The discovery that I can still say what
I want to say on men *and* women."

What are you looking for?

"For purity and simplicity."

What's one problem you are having
in your process?

"Not working in a linear way but out
of the tasks that Tedd is setting me."

What is your source material or
starting point?

"The grip of a wrist."

thirtythree

An observation: !

Paul's movements comprise big shapes and subtle gestures. They create a striking, gentle dissonance. He keeps the space open, roomy, cleansed.

Paul's Reflection:

I could never have made a work like this even in 10 more years. I wouldn't have got this out in a space. Now I am obsessed with a task!

In finding the essence of a task. For example, I located 'the grip' as essential to the material and through the task of "essentialising" the grip,

all the material came from it. I got to the story or emotion of the piece but by a very different means. I have, according to Tedd, a "gesture / dance split".

The question / task Tedd sets for me is " How can Paul make gestural dance?".

Mary's Reflection:

Starting with movement and seeing what it says to me, staying with the "intelligence" of movement itself for longer rather than taking

off on "what it means"; busting open my habitual way of making. Material that I made was torn up again and again and I didn't mind

arriving at only one moment or one minute of material to look at. I reflected on the tasks more in the evenings and found I really

needed this before I could just go with it. I set up some of my own tasks as well.

Tedd's task: Stop conceptualising and look at the material.

What discovery does Mary make in the moment of attending to her material alongside the invited audience this afternoon at the showing? The audience is very inquisitive, very lively. Two sightings are emerging: the "sensuous surfaces" of the movement and the "humanity" of the movement. Tedd has set the material to two different pieces of music: the Kronos String Quartet and Uri Caine in a rendering of Mahler. Tedd uses music as a tool, as a set of extremes, as a lens through which to look, and as an information-gathering device.

Audience:

The Mahler makes the dancers 'react', promotes more sensuality between the dancers.

Audience:

The Mahler swamps the movement!

Audience:

The Quartet makes you have to go into the the world of the movement. The Mahler is too character-driven.

Audience:

The Mahler brings the movement to you.

Mary seems fascinated but also immobilised by the audience's response.

■ ■ ■ ...space (chora) which is eternal a

destructible,... which provides a position for everything that comes to be...

*Plato. Timaeus and Criticas, Trans. D. Lee, Harmondsworth: Penguin, 1971. Cited in Lehman, Hans-Thies.

"From Logos to Landscape: Text in Contemporary Dramaturgy.": *Performance Research* Vol 2, No. 1 1997.

All the figures shrugging, twitching, morphing in a multitude of subtle subversions. So many cross-cultural inferences infiltrate their bodies: Brechtian, Javanese, clowning, Vaudeville. Hands grasp the air, arms propel like blades spluttering out of control. Hands pray, then clutch while arms spread open and upwards like wings, exultant. Then things get really playful. The dancers wave, flag each other down like desperate hitch-hikers in infinite space. They point, they slash. Bodies like machetes. Two dancers perform Chaplinesque duck walks. Two others perform bumps and grinds. All execute quirky little feats of balance and make asymmetrical smudges around the space with their weight in their hips. Jake looks like he has "seen the light" and an enigmatic smile spreads across his face while he stares outward over our heads. Richard carries on busily through the space looking calm and determined, no matter what he has to do. Lisa and Ríonach fulfil one task after another with steadfast matter-of-factness.

Andy looks like an enormous tree with limbs spreading out in all directions. This piece is growing into a postmodern cabaret and the performers are filling the shapes of angels, clowners, joggers, gliders. An enormous amount of material here in a great growth spurt from week 2 to week 3. The dancers look like they know something about how to work. They exude concentration, serious playfulness, insight, discovery. Jake smiles uncharacteristically throughout his dancing. The choreography brings out a quality in him, he doesn't yet know. Mary's concerned that the material looks too random. Tedd thinks it's too closed up.

Mary:

I started afresh with this material amidst dancers' protests. I had held on to so much from my process - my old process - and I wanted truly to find new work, really work new.

Tedd:

Look at what the work is now ..... not what you were aiming for. You tend to work things to death, Mary. Let it be what it is. Look at it. Go with what it is showing you, offering you. Let the movement dictate the character, Mary.

Tedd:

The sadness that can be laughter, the subtlety of clowning, so lovely a quality in this material. In this choreography you work with juxtaposition. The two dimensional flatness of the body with curvaceousness. That brings out humour.

Mary:

Oh, so you juxtapose movement against movement. That's a discovery... I am so fearful of being trivial.

Hope for trivia! Don't fear it!

Mary returns to her question:*

How can I lead if I am the most lost person in the world? I was really on unsure ground in this work; very traumatised, fearful. I made a hope and fear list.

The dancers said they found Mary's moment of being lost very frightening.

Mary:

I'm going to a place I've never been before. Of course I'm lost!

Tedd:

I felt a lack in myself for having the dancers respond this way, for not having got them to accept lostness, or a letting go on Mary's part.

Mary:

I needed to learn how to be lost but still be driving the piece, still be "in control". I still need to learn this.

The dancers kept insisting they were "just bodies", that they were not going on the journey, that where they come from it is a coping mechanism to alleviate or avoid the trauma of process.

Tedd:

I should have told the dancers that in a research project like this you need to let the choreographer go anywhere. This kind of project is very hard on the dancers. For three weeks they go through everything, then drop it, then go through everything, then drop it, etc. This process of working, this kind of project, is a working culture that they need to be much better prepared for. I wanted to bring them (the dancers) with me but I was intimidated by them. I didn't know that at the start.

Acknowledge that you are being judged.

Tedd: Do not judge.

Ríonach:

The dancers must be non-judgmental but it is a strange process. One mentor, two choreographers ...... It is a strange process. When you are working on product you need to judge. Here, whatever the choreographer wanted to do you did without judging. I think the next work they do will show all this process. The choreographers at this stage in this project seemed to focus on cleaning up and clearing up their intentions and how to communicate that, more than on developing new vocabulary. In this project we didn't ask, "Is this an interesting piece?" but rather, "Is that what you mean?" It required a kind of detachment, not from the tasks or towards the choreographers but rather towards the work itself.

Lisa:

To work for process not product. When you are in a company you are constantly working towards a piece and it's all very competitive. Here there is less pressure. It's more equal. It's about material and less about who has got what ....On one of the "No Talking Days" we stuck to the tasks that Paul had been given. There was tension and then explosion because Paul didn't stick to this. Then there was a bit of clearing the air from this.

Ríonach:

Working with two completely different choreographers: different capabilities, different approaches, comparing and contracting information, insight. A way to think about process. Our raw material in dance is people. So how are choreographic ideas communicated to people? The people dialogue is so interesting, so vital. Mary's body, for instance, communicates much more effectively than her words. I want to tell her "stop being so fuzzy". Paul's work is personal, so I felt I needed a relationship with him for me to get into his work. With Mary I could communicate directly through movement.

Ríonach & Lisa:

Our advice to other dancers coming into this project would be: Patience, No Expectations. The project is not about a dancing experience. It is mentally stretching rather than physically. You can't go down your own path. You must accept the context.

Jake:

Should the dancers simply facilitate the choreographer? What is their effect on the mentor? The dancers need feedback from the mentor and the choreographers need more security from the set-up. Are they uncomfortable about 'failing'? Is there an issue about judgement by the dancers?

Richard:

Your role as a dancer is diminished. The choreography is a very fragile process. We must be very sensitive to that. We must stand back, look, observe, remove ego. Different levels of awareness come into the space. Some choreographic changes may be very subtle. There is a lack of continuity in this exploration process. The dancer can't get attached to the work because it will keep changing. 'My' movement is gone the next day etc. There are "good" days and "bad" days regarding flatness or challenge. There is an embodying of two different styles simultaneously …. difficult. We must remember that we are witnessing the ways in which choreographers take on mentor's notes. We are not seeing the choreographers at their "best".

Andy:

If you can't do process this project is not for you. Nothing is product here. All is ongoing. For the dancer I would advise: choose 3 tasks personally for your own growth, one per week. The dancers need performance tasks!

Ríonach:

As dancers we felt very aware of the needs and challenges for the choreographers. Could Tedd have pushed the choreographers further? Turned their tools of process upside down? We had little involvement in the dialogue between Tedd and the choreographers …. we weren't necessarily privy to the aims of each day.

Tedd does not agree that there should be feedback or dialogue between dancers and mentor.

Dancers are not
choreographers.
Dancers can show the
choreographer where
something can go.
The choreographers can use
this information but they
should not be
driven by it.

Tedd

See how the dancers hotten up, give the material their attention, clarify, punch and carve stuff out of the guts of the space to bring it kicking and screaming into the world. I start to wish I hadn't talked to the dancers at all during the making process. I prefer the non-knowing state, the state of innocence to view them in. I am fascinated to see their qualities mark and etch the space, impress something in my way of seeing the dance, watch their faces, their decisions, their breathing, their playing. I want the myth of the dance and dancers. I have my favourite moments in this material. Jake sitting on Richard, arranging his hands, while Ríonach and Lisa behind them shadow their moves. Having favourite moments is the gift we are offered. We store these moments in our body house for living. This is why I look at dance and this is what life is about - being ready to receive the gifts.

Observation of a run-through of material

29 January (week 3): Tedd's Morning Class

The pianist hasn't turned up, Tedd has lost the key to the video and CD cupboard. He counts out the phrase, moving all

the while in his black robes, bare feet, bright yellow band-aid on his heel. The class has a classical grounding: brushes,

tendus, piques, pliés. The pianist arrives. Tedd demonstrates a lovely new combination: 1st position, pulsing jumps

in place, then jumps in 2nd, then in changing 5ths, then slides in open 4th with changes across the floor. I start to feel low

after the class. It's 11.45. The dancers are working with Mary on material.

What am I doing here? Why am I writing this? I am in back pain and getting a sty.

in my eye. These are completely alien ailments for me. What is my body telling me?

That I should be moving across that floor? Choreographing something?

Not documenting something that can never be captured?

Hello Diana...

Hope you are well and not too overworked. Take a half hour, and go for a walk by yourself, sit down under a tree and for that half hour, know that you cannot do anything about any of the thoughts or feelings that you have because you are sitting under that tree or walking and that is all you can do at this time. That short period of time of knowing that you cannot possibly do anything about the things that have to be done and accepting that fact, can do very good things. Notice everything that is green, each thing that is green. It is only a half hour and will not make any difference to your work load. Believe me! Haha! ......

Tedd!

space, inescapable and all-sus

ning space, is our unrecognised god

nson, Tim. "On the Cultivation of the Compass Rose" in *Setting Foot on the Shores of the Connemara & Other Writings*. Dublin: The Lilliput Press, 1996. Cited in Walker, Linda Marie. " In the Midst of Many: The Butcher, his Lover, her Husband, and the Hit Man" *Performance Research* Vol. 3, No. 2 1998

A rehearsal of Paul's material

The dancers have only worked in silence. Tedd informs them that there will be music this time and that it will feel odd. It's Noh music. "I'm going to be playing with the sound so don't take cues from me", he says.

Silence. Richard propels himself through the space on his back, as though mopping the floor with the bristles of his vertebrae. You could hear a pin drop. Stillness. The other dancers are in a clump, not moving. Then they exchange looks. A shoulder dips, a torso curves, someone pliés, someone turns. The clump starts to open out and travel across space. The dance is quiet, introspective. There are little pockets of space where dancers simply sit or stand and observe one another. Others observe their own hands. Richard plays with the weight of Jake's hand then Jake plays with the weight of Richard's head. The Noh music is sparse, serene, spacious. Dancers keep watching other dancers and soon a dialogue builds – a doing-watching dialogue. I wonder what the dancers are thinking as they sit, performing stillness, watching each other.

Music: Hayashi Music of Noh, Tsuxma Pan Music and The John Cage Tribute/A Chance Operation

A post-rehearsal coffee break with Rionach and Lisa:

Paul's work:

At first it was so tentative and so intense. In week 2 there was significant expansion of movement repertoire. In week 3 no more "gestures" but rather full body gesture. He became more forceful, more to the point. Surely this was good for him. I felt more and more willing to get involved. He was making the piece more and more complex.

A coffee break with Tedd:

Paul's process has been cool, methodical, many notes and much journal writing.

Sharing material with the invited audience:

Paul:

One of my tasks was to work on a solo with Jake. Tedd asked me what the most interesting choreographic moment was in that material. Answer: "the grip". This became the information for moving the piece on, for digging into the material. The bones of a piece emerged and in the two weeks of distilling, I came to see that this piece brings me back to what I do/did before now, perhaps, but in a much more human landscape.

I was intrigued to see what would happen next in the material. So much material was generated from one idea (task), from trusting in the task I was given. That's not ME. It's material.

I don't recognise myself in it – my familiar choreographic characteristics. The work with Tedd showed me something I didn't know. Now what? What/where/how do I go from here? I am so pleased with what I feel has been a huge breakthrough for me and that I could watch this material open up without censoring, without worrying.

Changing Paths:

Paul is a choreographer of men. Inside this laboratory he works with women for the first time.

"Seeing my ideas on women's bodies was much more interesting than I realised. Now I have less thinking time and more doing time. Now, my bluff has been called! After Week 1 I was saying No! I can't do this! But now I feel very free from the agenda I had set myself before. Before I was thinking 'remedies'. Now I trust that I can open something out.

This could not have happened in my usual process of making work. I have to use my history to draw on, to solve with, to produce from – the constraints/tasks I've been given. I've kept a log of everything in this process. I've been very disciplined about writing through this. A huge problem for me about doing this project has been the question: Will I lose my unique (choreographic) traits?"

THE RESPONSIBILITY OF LEARNING SOMETHING NEW*

Moment with Mary:

I want to try working with just movement rather than starting with an emotional or dramatic theme. The challenge for

me was not to quickly respond to the drama revealed to me in the movement but to allow the movement to reveal

itself more. By the end of week 2 I felt I still hadn't broken from my background and I decided that I didn't care if

I only ended up producing one minute of new vocabulary. In week 3 I started all over again – to find out what it is this

material is revealing

...... forget the concept and see the material.

An observation by Tedd:

She handled the tasks well on the day. In the end the work came together, but she may rebound into old habits.

She needs to develop more trust in order to get closer to her movement vocabulary. For example, an exploration

of arm movements led to jumps and jumps led to travelling. She got started by the tasks but grew when she trusted the

tasks, rather than working as in extension from the last piece.

*Adrienne Brown. See Appendix 2

only 3 weeks only 3 weeks

only 3 weeks only 3 weeks

only 3 weeks only 3 weeks*

*Fragment of a dancer's notebook

a dancer's question*

My role as a dancer is to facilitate the proces

Do I facilitate the task as set by the mentor?

Do I interpret the task according to my experience as a dancer

Do I follow the choreographer's interpretations?

*Jake McLellan. See Biographies

Hi Tedd

      MORE ON AN EARLIER QUESTION: I hear from Mary that while you were in residence at FC
you met with the dancers on a daily basis, without the choreographers ......

Hello Diana

      ......This is true. With the experiences that I have had with the dancers
I thought this might be a good method of keeping them informed, and they in turn keeping
me informed of how they were and any suggestions they might have for more efficiency in the
working process. The dancer discussions were more on a level of finding out from their
perspective how the choreographers were doing and if there were difficulties, could there
be a way of alleviating them. I tried not to allow these discussions to become too complaint
oriented, but tended, hopefully, to guide them towards a constructive process of "what needs
to be done to correct this".

I wasn't always successful in my dealing with the dancers but I think that the meetings made them
sense that they were a part of the process and had a say in what was going on. Other topics
discussed included advice on what to do in the studio to help the choreographers out of a block.
This came up a few times. I usually advised against following one's normal tendencies (to offer so
many solutions that the choreographer gets disoriented and distanced from their original idea).
But each choreographer is different and each block is different.

email

We also discussed some problems that dancers had with each other. It was really
just an open forum to as honestly as possible deal with the problems of humans
working together under imposed conditions of creativity (that is,
choreographers had assignments, dancers were told what to do by the
choreographers, creation is not a democratic process)....

From Andy Papas' Notebook

"Surely part of the RD project should be to teach the choreographer how to deal with the comments made by dancers ... (that's the) honest, hardworking and quick thinking professional world of contemporary dance...... it would have been more realistic had all the dancers been encouraged to speak their own minds."

A problematic, lively, unresolved issue
An ever shifting set of negotiations
A space of politics, histories, emotions
A deeply articulate space

HE DANCER IN RELATION TO THE CHOREOGRAPHER AND MENTOR

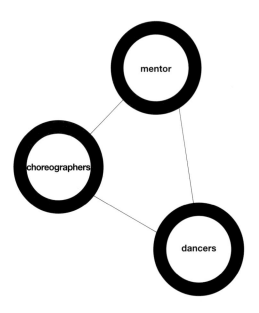

a question

Mary, Paul, in this 3 weeks of 'finding out' process, do you feel you have gone far enough? What do you dare to think of as the limits of your personal experimentation?

Paul:

I can only do what I really can do. That's as far as I personally could go.

Mary:

It's to do with the art form. It's not like throwing paint against the walls, you're dealing with dancers. It's a medium you're negotiating. How do I get what's in here (in me) out through them? It's a very vulnerable process. With film rushes you can keep looking at it, reflecting on it. I learned about the experience of the dancers and their judgement in this process. Tedd says not to judge our work as we are working on it but the dancers are judging it all the time!

Tedd:

The dancers' sensitivity needs intensifying and this can aid the choreographers in their process.

Mary:

You have to consider the readiness of the dancers to show the material…. the dancers need to digest the material…. they may not get it.

Tedd:

We have to consider the safety of a human being. No one was injured in this process.

Ríonach:

It was good swapping choreographers. But I question the sharing. It takes up too much energy. First week the work gets broken down. Second week we do risky, lovely explorations. Third week is focused on the sharing. We might have got further if we didn't think about showings. How much further would/could the choreographer have gone? We got absorbed in structuring, remembering.

A question:

What would it be like if you went through this process for three weeks, working on material, dropping it, working on material, dropping it etc., ….. never seeing where it might go…… what would that feel like? (not to produce a showing?)

A question:

What would happen if all the dancers went much much further in the material, took each moment to the limit, extended all the lines? You, Mary, keep using the term "over the top". Well, why don't you go over the top and see what happens? Richard, every time you performed a particular sequence it seemed to get bigger. What would happen compositionally if every dancer went as far as possible? How could your delivery alter the structure? What did you come away with after three weeks compositionally?

a question…

Mary:

I've always felt like seeing the dancers go way over the top then pull back….finding the extremes, seeing more of the chaos.

Richard:

I saw many changes in the work.

Mary:

The dancers can change your work… A painting doesn't change but dancers do, so your work will look different.

Paul:

I definitely saw new performances of my material in front of the audience.

Mary:

Personally I'm not happy with the 'showing' model. What's it achieving? It interrupts the flow of the process. It disrupts experimentation. Paul, I know you do a lot of sharings as part of your process. But I'm not sure about it…. the audience didn't have very many questions…… and there never are.

Tedd:

Don't expect the audience to ask questions. That's not what they're there for. If you want them to ask questions then the choreographers have to frame the questions for them, have specific questions they want to ask the audience.

Paul:

I value the interaction in the sharings even if the audience do not ask many questions.

Mary Brady:

Yes, I have questions about the sharings too. No matter how you diffuse the material, it's still a formal process.

Tedd:

Imagine Tuesday, no showing, Wednesday, no showing, Thursday, no showing…. I'm not sure, but I think you get a little bit extra with the dancers …. it's a clarifying for the choreographer. I would think you saw things…..

Mary:

Of course I did!

Mary Brady:

But do you always have questions when you put up an artwork or a piece of theatre? I think there's something forced about it.

Mary:

I saw Paul's work much more clearly today, but in my own experience I was getting down to crafting when I was really just discovering something new. I resorted to stuff I'd used before. I didn't stick to my "one minute of new material is enough" plan.

Tedd:

You told me that you would take something and drive it and drive it and drive it until you could see where it might go….

Mary:

The pressure of showing made me "back pedal".

Ríonach:

I'm not sure showing our process to the audience is the right thing to do.

Mary

I thought the sharing produced too much of a change in the work…..

Mary Brady:

Maybe you could have opted for the "one minute only" of new material.

Mary:

I kept thinking, "The audience came all the way from Dublin… I have to show them more…." I should have shown them fragments rather than a whole stretch of material.

Tedd:

That was my influence. I love it…. risking to show the whole stretch.

Diana:

Also a lot of material emerged! You could celebrate the sheer mass of material you've accumulated in three weeks – let it run, have a good look at it… It has this organisation at the moment, this structure, this dynamic, this journey. Both pieces clearly showed journeys. In Paul's piece the dancers even sat and observed/watched each other's journeys…..

Tedd:

In the process we discussed how you were communicating your ideas. After the sharing where do you go? Observing these post-sharing moments are very valuable. What are you seeing when the audience is there?

Mary:

I was totally obsessed with how every move was done in the first place. Tedd said "Just get it out, get the material out". I said, "I can't". There's a whole 'presence' thing in it. They evolved from pure movement into 'characters' and I let that come in. The most exciting thing was the compositional daring that was starting to go on.

Diana:

Will the dancers who have worked with you here be of help when you return to your company to work with them?

Mary:

No, I'll have to rely on myself and on very rigorous dialogue. Dancers' dialogue can be problematic….. Our relationship has deepened, some things have broken through/down and these will inform the next steps… things will settle. But I don't know what 'the work' is! I don't know what people are talking about when they talk about 'the work'. There are still so many decisions to be made about the work and I don't feel at all sure how to make them.

Tedd:

May I advise that you drop the work you've done ….leave it alone….start afresh because it brings all the baggage and the bewilderment back with it…. start new material.

Paul:

I can't over-emphasise the change in these three weeks for me ….a preciousness has gone from my working practice…..a big break through.

Mary:

I'm quite disorientated. I have no idea. I may be worse off now!! I need more 'therapy'. I could use three more weeks of this. I'm fearful that I'll slip back into my other practice.

Mary Brady:

You're welcome to come back and not get back into the production line.

he puritan ethic under which
e continue to live and struggle
o matter how many times it is
pointed out – already perceives
t-making as play and pleasure..
hich it is and
uch a notion...
so a serious,
ngaging, form
ommitment ar
uritan qualities
e paramount,
nd dancers are
cknowledge al
ey cannot ma
ances.

The puritan ethic under which we continue to live and struggle – no matter how many times it is pointed

out – already perceives art-making as play and pleasure which it is and refuses to support such a notion....

Art-making is also a serious, and seriously engaging, form of work in which commitment and discipline

– two puritan qualities if ever there were – are paramount. Choreographers and dancers are forced

to acknowledge and practice both, or they cannot make or perform dances.*

*Alexander, Elena. *Footnotes: Six Choreographers Inscribe the Page*. Gordon & Breach International, 1998.

COMMENTS BOX

Andy Papas' Notebook

"Well organised by Firkin Crane, nice space, great working hours, fine accommodation, slightly underpaid, wonderful bunch of dancers.... Mary inspiring, Paul intriguing, Tedd understanding ....best way for things to improve is to secure funding for this project on a regular basis."

"As dancers there are second-long "bleeps" of ecstasy. These moments are few and far between. Pedestrians will never understand this feeling . These moments come, like love, when you least expect it. So, you can have these drugs in a class, a Righting Dance Project, or a performance. These "bleeps" are what keep us going."

Hi Diana   4 May 1999

I have emailed Mary and Paul

recently to see how they are and

what effects the lab has had,

if any. They have not responded

as yet. Perhaps, a little

insecurity, but I wondered if

it had had any effect at all.

Both Mary and Paul were quite

exhausted by the end, I think.

So the last few days I am not

sure of exactly how much they

actually took in.

...........Tedd

How does the Righting Dance project promote choreography as research?

How can the project stimulate interest in the 'tracking' of choreographers' processes and evolution as artists?

How does the project initiate dialogue on documentation for choreography?

How can the concept of performance research be developed and communicated to funding bodies and the dance community? **How can the 'controls' for the project be explored and developed?**

How to select the dancers?

Should choreographers work with dancers they do not know?

Should dancers be familiar with the choreographer's work before participating in the project?

Should there be more than one choreographer at a time?

Should there be a Righting Dance 'core' of dancers or a 'lab' company

Should dancers only participate once in this project or lab, or should the participation be ongoing? **Could the project create longer term teams of choreographers and mentors working togethe**

Could the mentor return to 'edit' and assist the choreographer in the development of the work towards public production?

How can this project assist dancers and choreographers towards genuine cross-artistic dialogue about th art form and not just about funding? **What are Irish choreographers drawing from, for their work?**

Is there a body culture in Ireland? How can choreography become more valued as a discipline within this culture?

dialoguedocumentationdisseminationdebate

A piece may be worked on for months,

for a year or years, then performed

rarely, and never seen

again....those who make dances,

those who dance them, are most

often unwittingly akin to Buddhist

monks who spend inordinate time

making intricate, multicoloured sand

paintings, only to sweep them away.

The makers and doers of dances accept

this exigent reality, accept writing in

empty space, accept impermanence,

though not without the barrier of hope.

They continue their investigations,

even as time simultaneously exists

and disappears, a slow and

constant link ......"

*Alexander, Elena,ed., *Footnotes: Six Choreographers Inscribe the Page*. Gordon & Breach International, 1998.

MARY BRADY is Artistic Director of Firkin Crane. She has worked extensively in areas of dance theatre and dance education, both in the North and South of Ireland. She served as a member of the Executive Committee of the Dance Council for five years and is currently a member of the Arts Council of Ireland.

PAUL JOHNSON is a choreographer and Artistic Director of MaNDaNCE. He trained at the Laban Centre in London and has worked as a performer, teacher and choreographer throughout Ireland, England, Scotland and Europe. Currently he is Choreographer-in-Residence at the Project Arts Centre in Dublin, the first such appointment in Ireland.

LISA Mc LOUGHLIN trained at the Rambert School of Ballet and Contemporary Dance in London. She performs in Ireland with the Daghdha Dance Company and with Rex Levitates.

JAKE McLELLAN trained at the Ballet Rambert School of Ballet and Contemporary Dance in London. He has performed and taught for a wide range of companies and choreographers including Motionhouse, Wayne McGregor, Janet Smith, Lloyd Newson, Gregory Nash, Shobanagh Jeyasingh, Dance Theatre Red and many others.

RÍONACH NÍ NEILL trained in contemporary dance and ballet at the Laban Centre and the Royal Academy of Dance in London (supported by the Arts Council and Dublin Corporation bursaries). She performs in Ireland with Daghdha Dance Company and New Balance Dance Company. She has served as dance artist-in-residence in the Connemara Gaeltacht and has recently been awarded an Arts Council bursary to study choreography in New York. She holds a PhD in Geography.

MARY NUNAN is founder member and Artistic Director of Daghdha Dance Company. Her choreography has been performed throughout Ireland and at international dance festivals in Berlin, Munich, Paris, Barcelona and London. In 1997 Mary collaborated with film director Donal Haughey to produce a screen adaptation of her dance theatre work TERRITORIAL CLAIMS, which was premiered at the Cork Film Festival and selected for screening at the Lincoln Centre's Dance for Camera Festival in New York. She was recently appointed to the MFA faculty in Dance at the University of Limerick.

RICHARD O'BRIEN trained with the Royal Ballet School and the Royal Academy of Dancing in London and graduated with First Class Honours from the Dance Theatre BA programme at the Laban Centre in London. He has exhibited video dance work at the Cochrane Theatre, performed in choreographic programmes at London's The Place and has been choreographic assistant to Jennifer Jackson. Currently, he performs with Daghdha Dance Company.

ANDY PAPAS originally studied Graphic Design before completing a degree in Dance at the London Contemporary Dance School. He has performed with Reinhid Hoffman Dance Theatre Bochum, DV8, AMP and in various Operas. From 1994 to 1998 he formed, and was Artistic Director of, Dance Theatre Red which performed in Resolution, Evolution, and Spring Loaded in Slovenia, Japan and in the UK.

TEDD SENMON ROBINSON has performed, produced and choreographed works for major festivals, companies and institutions throughout Canada and internationally. He was Artistic Director of Contemporary Dancers, Winnipeg from 1984 and Artistic Director of the Festival of Canadian Modern Dance in Winnipeg from 1985-1990. He has since been working as an independent, award winning choreographer and teacher nationally and internationally. He resides in Ottawa. The Venerable Tedd Senmon Robinson shuso is a monk of the Northern Mountain Order, Hakukaze Soto Zen.

DIANA THEODORES is a Reader in Theatre at Dartington College of Arts in Devon, England. She is author of First We Take Manhattan: Four American Women and the New York School of Dance Criticism, and many other writings on dance. From 1984 -1992 she was Dance Critic for The Sunday Tribune and directed the movement course at the Samuel Beckett Centre, Trinity College, Dublin. She has been chairing a forum series called "Conversations on Choreography" in Amsterdam and Barcelona and next in Cork. She has been invited to launch a Writer-in-Residence project for 2000-2001 at Firkin Crane.

[Appendix 2]

A Righting Dance "Time Out" with Choreographer Adrienne Brown

Choreographer Adrienne Brown undertook the inaugural Righting Dance programme in 1997. Over a period totalling nine weeks Adrienne and her troupe of dancers have been experimenting under the guidance of her chosen mentor, Kim Brandstrup, Artistic Director of Arc Dance Company, London.

In 1999 Firkin Crane commissioned a new work from Adrienne Brown and invited Kim Brandstrup to assume the role of Director. The result "Colmcille" was premiered in Firkin Crane, Spring 2000, with a national tour in autumn 2000.

An integral part of Adrienne's move from research and development to production was the participation of Kim as director of her newly commissioned work. Firkin Crane is documenting the transition of Kim Brandstrup from mentor to director, reflecting the choreographer's changing relationship.

[Appendix 3]

Firkin Crane Dance Development Agency

Firkin Crane's role in dance development and research in Ireland has been significant and far reaching.

Originally the old Butter Market, situated in the historic Shandon quarter of Cork city, Firkin Crane's architectural shape - a rotunda - along with its more recently designed interior designation as a space for dance (incorporating studios, a theatre, seminar rooms, library/archive, and a suite of offices) has created a unique physical resource for Irish dancemakers.

Since 1996 FC has initiated, produced, and piloted programmes through its:

- Righting Dance programme - choreographic mentoring schemes, forums for critical debate, interdisciplinary projects, residencies, a points of contact series.

- International performance seasons incorporating new dance commissions, and thematic dance performance/seminar projects.

- Education and outreach projects which include Youth Moves to Dance, Older People in Dance, (OPID) and a Moving Age research project.

Firkin Crane has evolved into an institute for dance and choreographic research: engineering opportunities for developing dance as an art form; fostering innovative approaches to dance practice; and operating within wider spheres of related activity in Ireland and internationally, to communicate and test models of best practice.

Firkin Crane, Shandon, Cork, Ireland.